Food Webs

River Food Chains

Emma Lynch

Heinemann Library
Chicago, Illinois

Customer Service   888–454–2279

Visit our website at www.heinemannlibrary.com

Photo research by Ruth Blair and Ginny Stroud-Lewis
Designed by Jo Hinton-Malivoire and AMR
Printed in China by WKT Company Limited.

09 08 07 06 05
10 9 8 7 6 5 4 3 2 1

Library of Congress Cataloging-in-Publication Data
Lynch, Emma.
 River food chains / Emma Lynch.
  p. cm. — (Food webs)
 Includes bibliographical references (p.   ).
 ISBN 1-4034-5859-6 (lib. bdg. : hardcover) — ISBN 1-4034-5866-9 (pbk.)
 1. Stream ecology—Juvenile literature. 2. Food chains (Ecology)—Juvenile literature. [1. Stream ecology. 2. Food chains (Ecology) 3. Ecology.] I. Title. II. Series.
  QH541.5.S7L96 2004
  577.6'416—dc22

                        2003026201

Acknowledgments
The author and publisher are grateful to the following for permission to reproduce copyright material:
Ardea p. **17** (John Paul Ferrero); Corbis pp. **5** (David Muench), **10** (Adrian Arbib), **11** (Roger Wilmshurst; Frank Lane Picture Agency), **13** (Steve Austin/Papilio), **22** (Jeremy Horner), **26** (Layne Kennedy), **27** (Aaron Horowitz); Corbis/Webistan p. **24**; Heather Angel/Natural Visions pp. **7**, **12**, **18**; Nature Picture Library pp. **8** (Lynn M Stone), **14** (Niall Benuie), **16** (Anup Shah); NHPA p. **23**; Science Photo Library p. **25** (Mark Smith).

Cover photograph of a Nile crocodile reproduced with permission of NHPA /Martin Harvey.

Illustrations by Words and Publications.

The publisher would like to thank Dr Dennis Radabaugh of the Department of Zoology at Ohio Wesleyan University for his comments in the preparation of this book.

Contents

What Is a River Food Web? 4

What Is a River Food Chain? 6

Which Producers Live in Rivers? 11

Which Primary Consumers Live in Rivers? 13

Which Secondary Consumers Live in Rivers? 15

Which Decomposers Live in Rivers? 17

How Are River Food Chains Different in Different Places? . .19

What Happens to a Food Web When a Food Chain
Breaks Down? 22

How Can We Protect River Food Chains? 25

Where Are the World's Main Rivers? 28

Glossary 30

More Books to Read 31

Index 32

Some words are shown in bold, **like this**. You can find out
what they mean by looking in the glossary.

What Is a River Food Web?

All living things are **organisms**. **Bacteria**, **algae**, plants, **fungi**, and animals (including humans) are all organisms. Organisms are eaten by other organisms. Small animals get eaten by bigger animals, and then these are eaten by even larger animals. When large animals die, they get eaten by tiny insects, maggots, and bacteria. Even mighty trees die and rot, and are eaten by beetles, grubs, and fungi. If you draw lines between the animals, showing who eats who, you create a diagram called a food web. It looks sort of like a tangled spider's web!

The organisms in a river **habitat** are part of a food web. In food web diagrams, each arrow points from the food to the animal that eats it, from **prey** to **predator**.

This is a North American river food web.

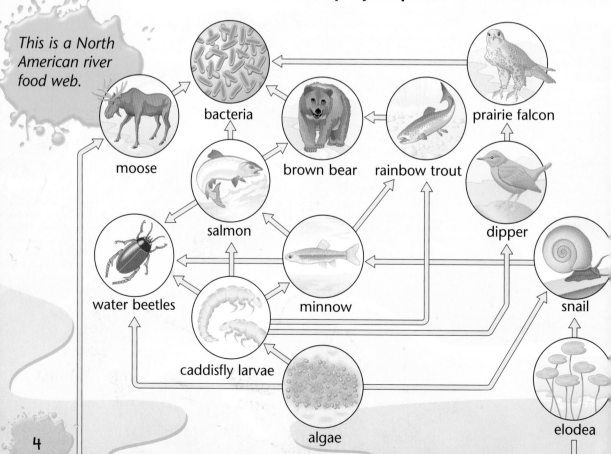

bacteria

moose

brown bear

rainbow trout

prairie falcon

salmon

dipper

water beetles

minnow

snail

caddisfly larvae

algae

elodea

What are river habitats like?

This book looks at the food web and food chains of river habitats. Rivers are large bodies of water that flow over land in long channels. They are found all over the world. Some, like the Amazon River, cover huge distances—the Amazon is over 4,000 miles (6,400 kilometers) long. Certain plants and animals live in river habitats because they are especially suited to life there. They are part of the river food web because the plants or animals they eat live in or around the river. Some, like fish, may live in the water. Some, like reeds and rushes, may grow along the river edges and banks. Some, like raccoons, may visit the river to look for food.

All rivers are home to a range of plants and animals that depend on each other for food and shelter.

What Is a River Food Chain?

A food web may look complex. but it is actually made up of lots of different food chains. Food chains are simpler diagrams. They show the way some of the **organisms** in a food web feed on each other. The arrows in the chain show the movement of food and **energy** from plants to animals as they feed on each other.

This is a North American river food chain. It shows how energy passes from one link in the chain to another.

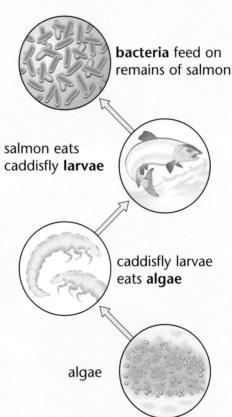

bacteria feed on remains of salmon

salmon eats caddisfly **larvae**

caddisfly larvae eats **algae**

algae

An organism can be part of more than one food chain if it eats more than one type of food, or if it is eaten by more than one other animal. Food webs in which organisms eat more than one food type are safer for the organisms within them. An organism that eats only one type of food will not survive if its food source disappears.

Starting the chain

Most food chains start with the energy that comes from the Sun. Plants trap the energy from sunlight in their leaves and use it to make their own food, in a process called **photosynthesis**.

Plants also take in **nutrients** from the soil through their roots and **carbon dioxide** from the air. Some river plants send roots into the mud on the river bed. Others float in or on the water. These may have little roots that hang in the water, or they may take in nutrients through their leaves. All plants use these nutrients, along with energy from food, to grow.

Every part of a plant can become food for animals in their **habitat**. They can eat the plant's roots, shoots, leaves, nuts, fruit, bark—or even the rotten plant when it has died. Without sunlight, all plants would die out. Then there would be no food for plant-eaters, and no plant-eaters for meat-eaters to eat, so most animals would die out, too. Sunlight helps to start all food chains by supplying the energy that is passed up each chain.

A plant's leaves are the factories where it makes food using energy from sunlight. The leaves grow in such a way as to catch the most light possible.

7

Making the chain

Plants are called **producers** because they trap the Sun's **energy** and make, or produce, food for other animals. Food chains usually start with plant producers. Producers provide food for plant-eating animals we call **herbivores**. In food chains, herbivores are the **primary consumers**. Primary consumers are often eaten by other animals known as **carnivores**. In food chains, these carnivores act as **secondary consumers**. Secondary consumers catch and eat primary consumers, but they may also eat other secondary consumers. Animals that eat plants and other animals are called **omnivores**. Omnivores may be primary consumers and secondary consumers.

Raccoons are true omnivores—they eat fruit, wheat, corn, birds' eggs, insects, and small river creatures such as this crayfish.

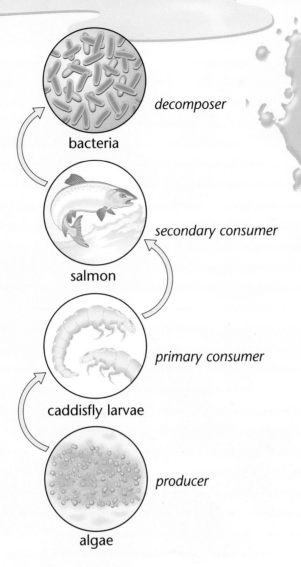

decomposer

bacteria

secondary consumer

salmon

primary consumer

caddisfly larvae

producer

algae

This food chain shows how energy passes from producer to consumers and decomposers.

More links in the chain

Food chains do not end when **organisms** die. After the death of an organism, **scavengers** such as worms and maggots eat its body. Then **decomposers** such as **bacteria** and **fungi** eat any dead remains that are left behind. The waste from these decomposers sinks into the soil or riverbed, where some of it becomes **nutrients** that can be taken in by plant roots. In this way, the chain begins again.

Breaking the chain

If some of the **organisms** in a food web die out, it may be deadly for others in the web. Sometimes natural events can damage a food web. **Droughts** may dry up a river, killing the animals and plants that live in the water. The birds and animals that live around the riverbank, feeding on its plants, insects, and fish, may also die. Human activity, such as **pollution** from farming and business, can also cause breaks in river food chains and in the cycles of nature, often with terrible results.

This river dried up during a drought, killing river plants and animals such as this crayfish.

Which Producers Live in Rivers?

Plants are **producers**, and they start most river food chains. There are many producers in a river **habitat**. Plants such as reeds and rushes grow along the river's banks. They provide places where water birds can build their nests. Some plants grow in the river itself. In fast-flowing rivers, the broad leaves and white flowers of water crowfoot can be seen above the surface. Below the water, long stems lead down to roots growing deep into the riverbed. These keep the plant from being torn up by the strong current.

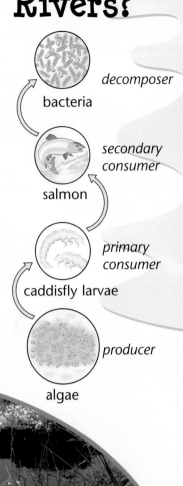

decomposer
bacteria

secondary consumer
salmon

primary consumer
caddisfly larvae

producer
algae

This bed of water crowfoot provides shelter for water snails, shrimp, and insect **larvae**.

Very tiny plantlike **algae** are also important producers in rivers. They float in the water and are eaten by small creatures like water fleas. The fleas then become food for insects and small fish. Slimy algae grow on the rocks and pebbles at the river bottom, and are food for insects and water snails.

Water fleas are tiny relatives of shrimp and crayfish. They feed on algae, and are food themselves for some insect larvae and fish.

Breaking the Chain: Producers

Green plants are very important to river food chains. In the 1960s, the Aswan dam was built to control the flow of the Nile River in Egypt. The dam has stopped the floods that used to bring rich **nutrients** to the fields around the river each year. Because the soil has become poorer, Nile farmers now use chemical fertilizers to help their crops grow better. These chemicals wash from the fields into the river, where they are taken in by the plants. The Nile is also **polluted** by nearby businesses and by boats for tourists.

Much Nile plant life has died or been poisoned. Animals in the food web, such as crocodiles and catfish, have died from taking in these poisons. Work is under way to clean up the Nile and control the pollution, but the yearly floods will never come back.

Which Primary Consumers Live in Rivers?

River **primary consumers** are often **invertebrates** like freshwater shrimp, water lice, water beetles, and insect **larvae**. The larvae of caddisflies live in rivers all over the world. They protect their soft bodies from **predators** by building shells from sand, tiny twigs, and even the empty shells of water snails. Most caddisfly larvae scrape algae off of pebbles with their front legs to collect and eat, but some **species** also eat animals, making them **secondary consumers** as well.

Snails and other **mollusks** such as river limpets also graze on water plants and algae. Tadpoles nibble at plant matter in the first few weeks of their life, but when they get bigger, they become secondary consumers and will also eat other small animals.

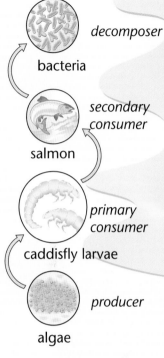

decomposer
bacteria

secondary consumer
salmon

primary consumer
caddisfly larvae

producer
algae

A caddisfly larva uses plant pieces or bits of gravel stuck to its shell as a disguise to fool predators.

Some **primary consumers** do not live in the water. Water birds such as ducks swim on the surface, diving to the riverbed to eat plants and **algae**. Water voles dig long tunnels in the muddy riverbanks to hide from **predators**.

Larger consumers

Beavers are large **rodents** that build dams across rivers. With their huge teeth, they gnaw down small trees to make their dams. The dams are usually about 80 feet (25 meters) long, but can be up to 1,650 feet (about 500 meters)! The dam traps water, creating a deep, calm lake. In the middle of the lake, the beavers build a wooden home called a lodge. Beavers eat bark, shoots, and small young trees. They even store branches under the water to eat in winter, when the lake ices over and they are trapped in their lodge.

Primary consumers can be very large. Moose wade in rivers to eat juicy water plants and escape biting flies. Where the Amazon meets the sea, manatees swim slowly along, feeding on underwater plants. They can hold their breath for over 15 minutes.

This young water vole is feeding. Water voles nibble reeds, roots, and shoots with their sharp teeth.

Which Secondary Consumers Live in Rivers?

Carnivores and **omnivores** are **secondary consumers**. Carnivores hunt other animals. Animals are rich in **nutrients**, but not always easy to catch, so carnivores use a lot of **energy** hunting their **prey**. The most common secondary consumers in rivers are fish. Small fish like bullheads lie at the bottom of the river beneath stones, waiting for young fish or insects to swim by. Then they dart out and gobble them up with their large mouths. Bigger fish, such as salmon sometimes hang almost motionless in the open river water, swimming against the current, and waiting to grab larvae or insects that swim by.

Other common river carnivores are birds. Herons, bitterns, and egrets hunt around near the banks of slow-moving rivers. They stand very still in the water, then quick as a flash they stab their beaks in the water and snap up small fish.

Larger carnivores also live in rivers. Otters have smooth, lean bodies, webbed feet, and broad tails, making them fast and talented swimmers. They eat fish, eels, crayfish, crabs, and frogs. They will even sneak into birds' nests and eat the eggs or chicks.

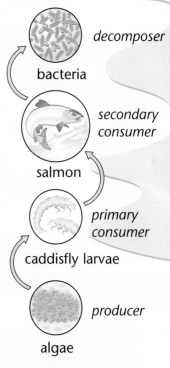

decomposer
bacteria

secondary consumer
salmon

primary consumer
caddisfly larvae

producer
algae

Breaking the Chain: Secondary Consumers

The Amazon River in Brazil is at risk from **habitat** destruction. Illegal loggers are cutting down the forests around the river, destroying animal homes and sources of food. Animals like the giant otter are now highly **endangered**. The giant otter has also been hunted for its soft fur and is now nearly **extinct**.

In hot countries, huge **carnivores** like crocodiles and alligators sun themselves on the riverbanks. The huge Nile crocodile can grow to 19 feet (6 meters) long and can attack large **prey** like water buffalo. Few animals would dare attack an adult Nile crocodile, but their babies are often eaten by other large **reptiles**, such as the Nile monitor lizard.

Great herds of gnus move across the eastern African plains in search of fresh grass. When a herd crosses a river, it provides welcome food for crocodiles.

Omnivores hunt for prey, but will also eat plants. Brown bears visit rivers to catch fish, frogs, or small **mammals**. They also look in the woods around the river for fruit, nuts, and small animals.

Which Decomposers Live in Rivers?

When plants and animals die, **scavengers** and **decomposers** recycle the decaying matter into simpler substances, such as **carbon dioxide** and water. This puts **nutrients** back into the **habitat** and gives plants the nutrients they need to grow, use the Sun's **energy**, and start the chains and web again.

Many scavengers live at the bottom of the river, hiding among rocks or pebbles or in the soft mud of the riverbed. Some, like the crayfish, are omnivores. They eat rotting plants, dead fish, or even small, live animals. **Herbivores** such as snails graze on weeds and rotting leaves and stems.

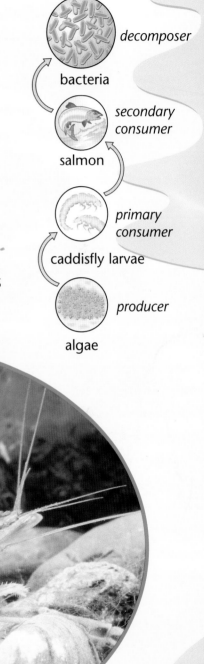

decomposer
bacteria

secondary consumer
salmon

primary consumer
caddisfly larvae

producer
algae

These shrimp eat the dead plants and animals that fall to the riverbed.

Animals that die in the river can be attacked by **organisms** such as flatworms. Flatworms can sense rotting flesh a long way away. They find the decaying organism and suck up its body matter with their long feeding tubes.

Flatworms eat dead plants as well as dead animals. This flatworm is on a decomposing leaf.

Decomposers such as **bacteria** and **fungi** break down dead organisms until they rot and break down. Some of the **nutrients** from the decayed organism fall to the bottom of the river. In fast-flowing rivers, many nutrients are carried away by the current. They may be carried a long way, until they reach the slower parts of the river. Slower parts of rivers often have muddier water and more animal life because the water is thick with nutrients.

How Are River Food Chains Different in Different Places?

NileFood chains can be very different from one river to another, or even along the length of one river. They are affected by the **climate**, the speed and depth of the water, and many kinds of human activity.

The Nile River

The Nile is the world's longest river, at about 4,132 miles (6,650 kilometers). It starts in the mountains of central Africa, then runs through deserts and swamps until it reaches the huge Nile Delta, where it flows into the Mediterranean Sea.

The thick roots of tall papyrus reeds slow down parts of the river, creating swamps where hippos gather. Pied kingfishers hide in the papyrus to watch the river, then dive down into the water to catch small fish.

Nile water shrews are common along the riverbanks. They are **prey** for the enormous Nile perch. Smaller fish are caught by fish eagles that swoop down from the sky. Nile crocodiles hunt the perch and other fish, including the catfish that turn upside down to feed on surface plants.

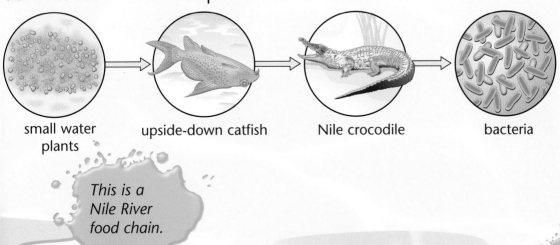

small water plants → upside-down catfish → Nile crocodile → bacteria

This is a Nile River food chain.

The Missouri–Mississippi River

The Missouri–Mississippi River is the second largest river system in the world. The Missouri and the Mississippi flow through the grasslands and marshlands of the central United States until they meet to form one mighty river. The river slows down, flooding its banks and forming areas of swampland until it finally enters the sea.

The slow, **nutrient**-rich river is ideal for plant life, and among the plants live thousands of crayfish. They feed on insects, snails, tadpoles, and rotting plants and animals. They are eaten by large salamanders called mudpuppies. Mudpuppies make a nice snack for the blue catfish, an animal that can grow up to 5 feet (1.5 meters) long. Small catfish are then at risk from the great blue heron.

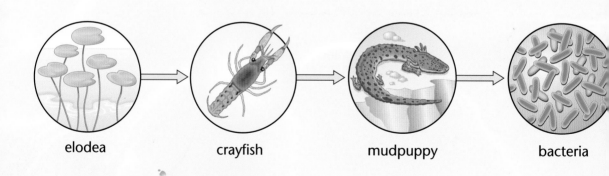

| elodea | crayfish | mudpuppy | bacteria |

This is a Missouri–Mississippi River food chain.

The Amazon River

The Amazon River in South America is the mightiest of all rivers. Every year in the rainy season, it gets even bigger, fed by the rains and melting water from the mountains. When it breaks its banks, nutrient-rich water floods the land for miles around, watering the Amazonian rain forest.

There are more **organisms** here than anywhere else on Earth. Lush plants grow along the banks and flood plains, forming forests and grasslands. The capybara, the world's largest **rodent** at a length of about 3 feet (1 meter), lives here. It is hunted by caimans and by large snakes called anacondas.

The river supports up to 3,000 different **species** of fish, including the world's largest freshwater fish, the arapaima. Tiny daphnia are eaten by angel fish. Their flat shape makes it easy for the angel fish to hide in the water weeds. Razor-toothed piranhas also swim here. They are **scavengers** and **predators**. A school of piranhas can strip a dead capybara down to the bone in less than one minute!

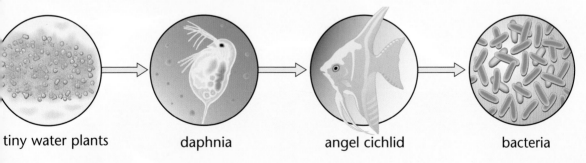

tiny water plants   daphnia   angel cichlid   bacteria

This is an Amazon River food chain.

What Happens to a Food Web When a Food Chain Breaks Down?

All over the world, river food chains and webs are at risk because of humans. Although much work is under way to stop more harm from being done, plants and animals in river **habitats** still face many problems today.

Pollution

The Nile and the Ganges rivers are badly **polluted** by chemicals from business, farming, and other waste. These poison the plants and animals, killing some of them and driving others away from their natural habitat.

The Ganges River is a holy river for Hindus, and thousands bathe in it each day, but its waters are dangerously polluted.

Habitat destruction

The Amazon rain forest is being destroyed as trees are cut down. This logging is destroying the habitat for wildlife. Animal numbers are going down because there is less cover to hide **prey** from **predators**. Without trees along the riverbank, there is less shade for river animals, and fewer leaves fall into the river as food for the fish there.

The spectacled caiman catches piranhas and other kinds of prey along the banks of the Amazon River.

Overhunting

Animals of the Amazon River are at risk from overfishing and overhunting. The red-headed turtle, spectacled caiman, and giant otter are all **endangered** animals, hunted almost to **extinction** for their fur, skin, or meat. Unless they are protected, they will be gone forever.

Dams

On the Missouri and Nile rivers, dams control how much water flows down them throughout the year. This limits the floods that damage businesses, but many river **species** rely on the natural way the water rises and falls during the year. On the Missouri, pallid sturgeon need high water flow to **spawn**, while least terns and piping plovers need low flow so they can nest on the banks. The numbers of all these animals have fallen in recent years, but there are now plans to make the dams copy some of the natural flows of the river.

The Nile River is choked with water hyacinths. In some places, beetles called weevils have been released among the hyacinth beds to control their spread.

Breaking the Chain: Unwanted Additions

Food chains can be broken if we introduce a new **organism** to a **habitat**. For example, travelers in the 1800s brought the water hyacinth from the Amazon to Africa. It was not part of the natural diet of any Nile animals, so it spread quickly. The water hyacinth can double its weight in twelve days, and grows faster than machines can cut it away. It has now spread to most of Africa's lakes and rivers. The huge mats it forms keep light and oxygen from reaching beneath the river's surface. This means that fewer types of fish are able to survive in the river. Water hyacinths affect fishing, water supplies, shipping, and power generation.

How Can We Protect River Food Chains?

All around the world, scientists, governments, and other groups are working to clean up and protect rivers and river food chains.

International research and protection

Scientists make surveys of river habitats. They test the water quality and **pollution** levels, and they keep track of animal and plant life around rivers to make sure that their numbers do not fall. In this way, scientists discover the links in the food web that need protection.

In the Amazon, scientists have discovered that gold mining and farming in the Andes Mountains may be harming fish **spawning** grounds. The young fish that hatch here **migrate** along the Amazon River. Destroying these spawning grounds would affect adult fish life thousands of miles downstream.

The tambaqui is a fish that lives in the Amazon River. It feeds on fruit and nuts that fall into the river.

Washing machines, refrigerators, barrels, and tires are among the huge piles of trash removed from the Mississippi by conservation workers.

Scientists suggest ways for governments to improve and protect river **habitats**. These ideas will help both the wildlife and the people who live along the river. Around the Missouri–Mississippi River system, laws have been passed to stop the use of some harmful chemicals in farming. Groups like Friends of the Earth, Greenpeace, and the World Wildlife Fund work to make sure that governments take care of rivers and to make the public aware of the problems. They try to prevent illegal logging near rivers and **pollution** from business and farming. They also suggest different ways of managing rivers in places where dams may be harming wildlife.

Conservation groups also run projects to teach people living near rivers, to make them more aware of how they can help to protect the rivers for everyone's future.

Research a river food web in your local area

You can study river habitats in your area. If you go on a trip near a pond or river, think about the food chains there. Here are some suggestions to help you find out about animal and plant life and some tips for protecting their habitats.

1. What is the habitat like? Is it cold or warm, shady or light?
2. Can you see any plants or animals? Put them in groups that are similar, such as plants, insects, birds, and fish.
3. What do you think each animal would like to eat?
4. Which are the **predators** and which are the **prey**?
5. Can you make a food chain of the animals and plants you see?
6. Think about how the habitat could change. How would the changes affect wildlife?
7. Do you see any signs of the habitat being polluted or destroyed?

We would all like to live near unpolluted rivers like this one. But even rivers in busy cities can be healthy habitats for animals and plants if people work to keep them free of pollution and trash.

Where Are the World's Main Rivers?

This map shows the locations of some of the world's biggest rivers.

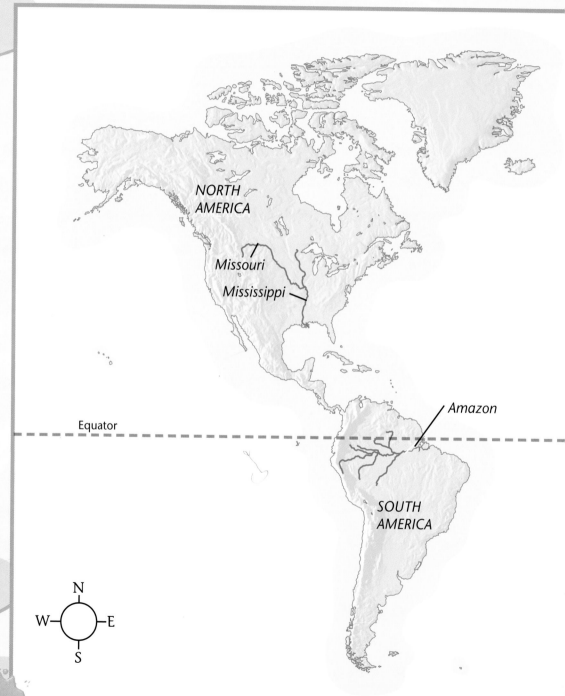

NORTH AMERICA

Missouri

Mississippi

Amazon

SOUTH AMERICA

Equator

N
W — E
S

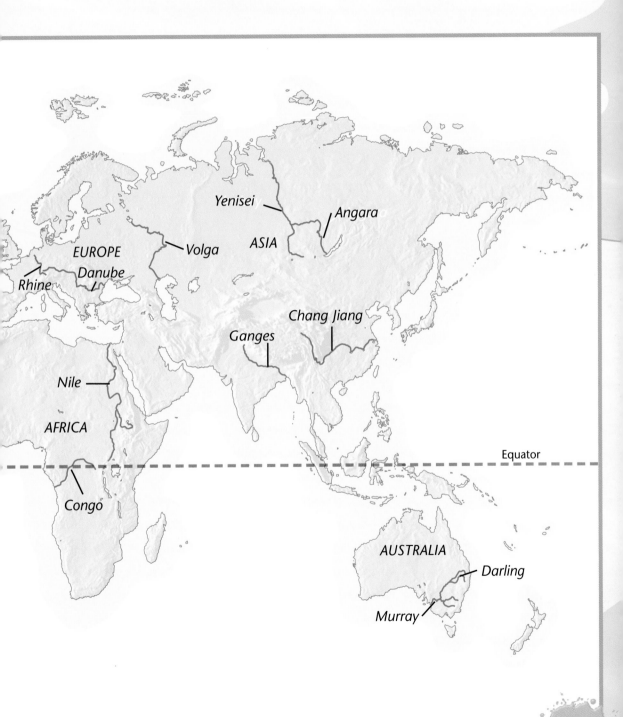

Glossary

algae (singular alga) small plantlike organisms

bacteria (singular bacterium) tiny living decomposers found everywhere

carbon dioxide gas in the air that animals breathe out and plants use to make food

carnivore animal that eats the flesh of another animal

climate general conditions of weather in an area

conservation protecting and saving the natural environment

consumer organism that eats other organisms

decomposer organism that breaks down and gets nutrients from dead plants and animals and their waste

drought long period with no rain

endangered at risk of dying out completely, as a species of animal or plant

energy power to grow, move, and do things

environment surroundings in which an animal or plant lives, including the other animals and plants that live there

extinct died out completely

fungi (singular fungus) group of decomposer organisms including mushrooms, toadstools, and their relatives

habitat place where an organism lives

herbivore animal that eats plants

invertebrate animal without a backbone

larvae (singular larva) young of some insects and other animals

mammal animals that feed its babies on milk from its own body

migrate to move to another place for part of the year, then back again

mollusk soft-bodied animal, often with a hard shell, such as a snail, oyster, or octopus

nutrient chemical that plants and animals need to live

omnivore animal that eats both plants and other animals

organism living thing

photosynthesis process by which plants make their own food using carbon dioxide, water, and energy from sunlight

pollution when chemicals or other substances that can damage animal or plant life escape into water, soil, or the air

predator animal that hunts and eats other animals

prey animal that is caught and eaten by a predator

primary consumer animal that eats plants

producer organism (plant) that can make its own food

reptile cold-blooded animal covered in scales

rodent mammal with large gnawing front teeth, such as a mouse or rat

scavenger organism that feeds on dead plant and animal material and waste

secondary consumer animal that
  eats primary consumers and other
  secondary consumers
spawn to produce its young as eggs
species group of organisms that are
  similar to each other and can breed
  together to produce young

More Books to Read

Baldwin, Carol. *Living by a River*. Chicago, IL: Heinemann Library, 2003.

Braun, Eric, and Sandra Donovan. *Rivers, Lakes, and Ponds*. Chicago, IL:
  Raintree, 2002.

Donovan, Sandy. *Animals of Rivers, Lakes, and Ponds*. Chicago, IL:
  Raintree, 2003.

Lauber, Patricia. *Who Eats What?* New York: HarperCollins, 2001.

Llewellyn, Claire. *Animal Atlas*. Santa Monica, CA: Creative Publishing, 2003.

Oxlade, Chris. *Rivers and Lakes*. Milwaukee, WI: Gareth Stevens, 2003.

Parker, Steve. *Pond and River*. New York: Dorling Kindersley, 2000.

Spilsbury, Louise, and Richard Spilsbury. *Plant Habitats*. Chicago, IL:
  Heinemann Library, 2003.

Squire, Ann. *Animal Homes*. Danbury, CT: Scholastic Library, 2002.

Index

algae 4, 6, 12, 13, 14
Amazon rain forest 21, 22
animals 4, 5, 8, 10, 13–16, 17,
   19–21, 22, 23

bacteria 4, 9, 18
beetles 13, 24
birds 14, 15, 19, 23
breaking the food chain 10, 12,
   15, 22–24

carbon dioxide 7, 17
carnivores 8, 15, 16
catfish 12, 19, 20
conservation groups 26
consumers 8, 12, 13–16
crayfish 10, 15, 17, 20
crocodiles 12, 16

dams 12, 14, 23, 26
decomposers 9, 17–18

endangered animals 15, 23
energy 6, 7, 8, 15, 17

fish 5, 15, 19, 20, 21, 22, 23, 24,
   25
food chains 5, 6–21, 22, 24
food webs 4, 5, 6, 22
fungi 4, 9, 18

habitat damage and destruction
   15, 22
   droughts 10
   logging 15, 22, 26
   overfishing 23
   pollution 10, 12, 22, 25, 26
herbivores 8, 17

invertebrates 13

larvae 11, 12, 13
nutrients 7, 9, 12, 15, 17, 18, 20,
   21

omnivores 8, 15, 16, 17
otters 15, 23

photosynthesis 7
piranhas 21, 23
plants 4, 5, 7, 8, 11–12, 22, 24
predators and prey 4, 14, 15, 16,
   19, 20, 21, 22, 23
primary consumers 8, 13–14
producers 8, 11–12
protecting food chains and webs
   25–27

raccoons 5, 8
reeds and rushes 5, 11, 19
river habitats 4, 5, 19–21
   Amazon River 5, 14, 15, 21, 23,
   25
   Ganges River 22
   Missouri–Mississippi River 20, 23,
   26
   Nile River 12, 16, 19, 22, 23, 24
rodents 14, 21

scavengers 9, 17, 21
secondary consumers 8, 13, 15–16
shrimp 11, 12, 13, 17
snails 11, 12, 13, 17
spawning grounds 23, 25